The
Faith in
Action
Series

Series Editor: Catherine Bowness

GW00390909

Building to Share

· ·

The Story of John Laing

Deborah Helme

Illustrated by Brian Platt

RMEP

RELIGIOUS AND MORAL EDUCATION PRESS

BUILDING TO SHARE

The Story of John Laing

Late one morning in 1949 a small, black car pulled into a cement works near Shoreham-by-Sea. It was a cold day with a sharp wind blowing in from the coast. A man, who looked about sixty, quickly climbed from the car. He pulled on a raincoat and followed the line of workers into the canteen for lunch. The canteen was in a temporary hut which was intended to last only a few months, until the cement works were finished. The roof was made of second-hand iron. In places it leaked, letting in rain and cement dust.

The man in the raincoat quietly took his tray of food and joined a group of workmen at a table. They hardly looked at him. Several minutes later one of the workmen said, 'Isn't the boss visiting the site today? I bet he's not sitting in this rotten

canteen eating this rubbish.' The men carried on talking until they had finished their meal and then went back to work. The man in the raincoat had said nothing but he walked thoughtfully to the site manager's office.

The manager and the office staff gave him a warm welcome – they had been waiting nervously for him all morning. They invited him to join them for lunch, explaining that they had arranged to eat in the comfortable, heated office building. The secretary had brought in a tablecloth and the cook had made something special. The man firmly refused the offer, saying he had already eaten in the canteen. Then he began to ask questions about the cement works and immediately everyone's attention switched to business.

The following day the canteen roof was repaired and the food seemed to have improved. This was the only clue to the cement workers that the man in the raincoat had been John Laing, their boss and the Chairman of the multi-million pound Laing Company.

By the time he was sixty, John Laing had turned a tiny family business in Carlisle into a huge, national building company. His company had been responsible for building some of the very first airport runways. It had built many schools, churches and hospitals all over the country and thousands and thousands of houses. After the Second World War, John Laing was even asked to advise the British and American governments on their housing policies. He had worked hard, his company had made millions of pounds, he could have been a very rich man – but he wasn't.

What Do You Think?

Important: In answering 'What Do You Think?' questions in this book, it is important that you not only state your opinion but also give as many reasons as possible for your opinion.

1. If you were in charge of a big company, what sort of car would you drive? Why do you think John Laing chose to drive an ordinary car?

2. What makes someone a successful business-man or business-woman? What do you think they need to be good at? What sorts of things do you think are important to them? What do you think motivates them to work hard?

3

School-days

John paused for a moment then scratched an answer to the final sum on the rough, yellow paper. He quite liked maths but he was terrified he would smudge his work. Paper was a luxury, and only the senior classes were allowed to use it. John's little sisters still had to write on slates in their lessons. John checked through his test paper and at the top in his best handwriting wrote, 'J. W. Laing, aged 12, May 1892'.

It was a warm Friday afternoon. John yawned and glanced around the classroom. His friends were still struggling on the last few questions, and occasionally one of them would dip their pen into the ink-well at the top of their desk. John knew he still had a while to wait until the bell rang at the end of the day. He thought about trying to get a book out from under the lid of his desk to read while he waited. He felt restless, he hated to waste time.

The classroom was a long, bare room but John liked it, because sitting at his desk he could just see a bit of Carlisle High Street. Sometimes he would spot his father's horse-drawn cart full of wooden beams or bricks going to a building site. His father was a builder. He wanted to be a builder too.

John began to imagine the day he would leave school and work with his father. He wanted the business to build big, important buildings. John was lost in his thoughts until the bell finally rang. The class rushed to the door and into the sunshine.

John walked home slowly with a group of his friends. Fridays were great, because he could look forward to the weekend. On Saturday he helped his father in the building yard and on Sunday the whole family would go to church together. He liked going to church, singing hymns and listening to people talk about God's love. After the service there was a Bible class where he could talk with his friends about stories in the Bible and ask questions.

While John was thinking about his plans for the weekend, his friends had started talking about

'automobiles' (cars). Six years earlier, in 1886, a German engineer called Gottlieb Daimler had invented the first roadworthy motor-car and he had been working to improve it ever since. All through Europe excitement about the motor-car was spreading, although few people had ever seen one. Some of John's friends thought that one day during their lifetime there would be motor-cars on the streets of Carlisle. Some of the others thought this was a crazy idea – almost as crazy as someone inventing a machine that could fly.

The discussion continued until the boys reached the end of St James' Road, where John lived with his parents and three sisters. John walked the rest of the way home on his own, hoping that one day he would see a motor-car and a flying-machine.

John lived in a small house similar to all the others on the street. None of the houses had electricity or gas and the toilet was in the yard outside. At night, when it got dark, the family would light oil-lamps so that they could read or play games together. They had no television to entertain them. The gramophone (an early version of the record-player or hi-fi turntable) had been invented several years earlier, but it would be a long time before families like the Laings would be able to afford one.

What Do You Think?

1. John looked forward to leaving school and becoming a builder. He was ambitious and wanted to build important buildings. What do you want to do? Do you have any ambitions? Have you thought of any ways you can fulfil these ambitions?

2. When John was a boy many things which we take for granted had not been invented. Can you imagine a world without cars, aeroplanes, televisions and CD players? Make a list of other modern inventions which the young John would not have known. Have all these items been good for the world or have some caused problems, e.g. global warming?

3. What kind of new and important things to help the world do you hope might be invented during your lifetime?

4. What do you do at the weekend? When John was twelve he liked going to church with his family, singing hymns and listening to people talk about Jesus. Does this surprise you? Give your reasons.

Disaster

John left school as soon as he was fifteen, like most young people at that time. He went to work in the small family business straight away. Before he could join his father managing the business in the office, he had to spend three years learning how to be a builder. This meant that he had to work long hours outside with the other workmen. He learnt to lay bricks, carry heavy loads and work in a team. Work started every morning at 6.30 a.m. The builders had to meet deadlines even if it was snowing or bitterly cold. John discovered that building was not an easy job.

In 1897, when he was eighteen, John began to work with his father in the office. His eldest sister, Annie, also worked there. She was the secretary and had to do all the accounting, note-taking and letter-writing by hand. Typewriters had already been invented and been on sale for over twenty years, but they were still too expensive for small businesses.

John was ambitious, he wanted his father to try building bigger and more exciting things. The Laing Company usually built houses and sometimes schools. John wanted them to expand and start to build factories or reservoirs or hospitals. Slowly he persuaded his father to try working on larger projects. The company built a reservoir in the Lake District which was a great success. John Laing's dreams had begun to come true.

On 6 September 1906, when John was nearly twenty-seven years old, he and his father signed a contract to build sewers by the docks in Barrow-in-Furness. John was very pleased that they had another chance to try a more challenging project. He carefully worked out how much the work would cost, how many men they would need and how long it would take.

However disaster struck. First the building site was flooded. Then they had to dig through quicksand. This was difficult and expensive. Sometimes one of the workmen would be caught by the quicksand and have to be pulled out, usually leaving his boots behind. These problems were bad, but then things got worse. The owners of the land where the sewers were being built objected to the work and took their complaints to court.

John was worried. He worked very long hours to supervise the work and encourage the men. Often he was too worried

or too busy to sleep. The sewers should have been built in a year. In the end, because the work was more difficult than first expected, it took over two years to complete them. The landowners took their problems from court to court trying to prove that the Laing Company owed them compensation. John and his father were afraid their company would run out of money and become bankrupt.

One day when John was feeling very depressed he went for a walk. He was so busy thinking about all his problems that he didn't notice where he was going. Lost in thought, he sat down on the side of a hill. Below him there was a beautiful view of Furness Abbey through a clearing in the trees, but John hardly noticed it.

He sat with his head in his hands and prayed. Throughout his problems he had often prayed: he believed that God heard his prayers and he trusted that God was in control. That day he

prayed, 'God, I have had enough. Because I've been so ambitious I have almost ruined the business and have worried my parents in their old age. I am sorry. Please show me a way through these problems. If the company survives I promise I will run the company differently in the future. I will think and pray about which projects to accept and pray you will guide me into making better decisions. Amen.'

John got up and looked around him for the first time since he had begun his walk. How had he missed seeing the beauty surrounding him? He never forgot the view from that spot or the prayer that he had prayed there.

A little while later the Laing Company won the court case. This meant that they did not have to pay compensation so they would have enough money to keep the business running. Instead of celebrating immediately with his friends and family, John quietly went back to the room at the Furness Abbey Hotel where he had been staying during the court case.

John remembered the promise he had made to God on the hillside. He found some hotel writing-paper and wrote down aims for his life. He decided to call this his 'Programme of Life'. There were two parts to it. First he decided that being a Christian was the most important thing in his life. This meant reading the Bible, praying to God and going to church would always be more important to him than his business. Secondly he decided that he wanted to make sure he enjoyed life and wanted to help others to enjoy life too.

At the same time, he thought about how he would spend his money. He decided that just because he might earn more and more money, he did not have to spend it on himself. He decided that he could live on a small amount and then give money away to people who were hungry, to charities and to his church. The rest of the money he would save and re-invest into the business or into charities. When John had finished writing down these plans, he read them over and over again until he had memorized them. Then he carefully folded up the writing-paper and put it inside his wallet. He decided that he would keep it in a safe place and look at it every year to check he always followed his new guidelines for life.

What Do You Think?

1. John was not always a successful business-man – he knew what it was like to have problems and to feel like a failure. Can you think of times in your life when things have gone wrong? Write down two or three words which describe how you feel when this happens.

2. How did John cope with his problems? How do you cope with problems?

3. John decided that if he earned a lot of money, he wouldn't spend it all on himself. He would give money away to churches and charities. Should people who earn high salaries give some of their money to the poor? Give reasons for your answer.

4. When you start earning money, how will you use it? Make a list of some of the things you might do with the money from your first full-time job. Which do you think are essentials and which are luxuries?

5. Have you ever helped to raise money or given money to charities? Charities or special appeals for funds are set up for many different purposes, e.g. research into cancer, caring for children, animal welfare. What sorts of charities do you think people should support? Give reasons for your selection.

6. What are the two most important aims you have for your life? If you were to write your 'Programme of Life', what would you put in it?

All Change

After the court case, John went back to work in the office in Carlisle. His father retired and John became responsible for managing the whole company. All around him things were changing. Often in the newspapers there was news of a new invention or discovery. People had even learnt how to build machines which could fly! In 1908, Samuel Franklin Cody made the first officially recognized flight in Britain.

The era of the motor-car was also coming closer. Frederick Lanchester made the first four-wheeler car in Britain in 1895. About ten years later Herbert Austin set up a factory in Birmingham. Motor-cars had come to Britain.

John noticed that people had begun to change their attitudes too. Ordinary people had started to stand up for their rights. Hard-working labourers realized that if they stuck together they could strike to get better wages and improve the way they lived. Many women too were unhappy and began to protest. They felt they had always been treated as second best to men and wanted things to change. These women thought they should be allowed to vote and joined together in hundreds to demand the right to vote and fairer treatment generally.

Whilst all these things were happening around the country, John continued to work hard in Carlisle. He was fascinated by the development of aeroplanes and motor-cars. He tried to imagine what it would be like to be able to move heavy building equipment in carts that didn't need horses.

In 1910 John's home life changed too, when he married Beatrice Harland, the sister of one of his best friends. Before they became engaged, Beatrice had read John's

John and Beatrice Laing at the time of their marriage

'Programme of Life' in which he had written about how he would spend his money and how he always wanted to keep his Christian faith as the most important part of his life. Beatrice was a Christian and very keen to live by these standards too.

John was very busy at work but he always found time for church activities. On Friday evenings young people from the church would come to a youth club in John and Beatrice's home, where they would play games and have fun. At this time there was not very much for young people to do. Several years earlier, Robert Baden-Powell had noticed this and had formed the Boy Scout Movement.

John and Beatrice were happily married for sixty-two years. They had two sons called Kirby and Maurice. If they ever had an argument or disagreement they would make sure that they had sorted out their problems before they went to sleep – this meant they could never be angry with each other for long. They got this idea from the Bible, which says: 'Don't let the sun go down on your anger.'

What Do You Think?

1. Despite their busy lives, John and Beatrice still found the time and energy to run a youth club. Why do you think they spent their free time doing voluntary work?

2. How do you spend your free time? Have you ever given up or been asked to give up your own time to help other people? What did you do or say?

3. Do you know any adults who run youth clubs or other activities in their spare time? Suggest three reasons why some adults do this.

4. Who do you argue with? How do you sort out these arguments? Do you think John and Beatrice's way of dealing with their arguments was a good idea? Would it be hard to keep to? Give reasons for your answers.

John and Beatrice Laing celebrating their Golden Wedding in 1960

War and Work

'Have you heard the news?' the grey-haired man behind the counter asked. 'We're going to war.' He'd been spreading the bad news all morning.

It was the beginning of August 1914 and Beatrice was in the local shop. She froze and felt a cold shiver run down her back. People around her had been talking about going to war for weeks, but she had never really believed it would happen. She felt dizzy and walked out of the shop in a daze, forgetting the bread and milk which she had intended to buy.

A short time later John signed up to fight in the war, but he never went to the battle on the front-line. His company was a 'red badge' firm. This meant that it had important work in Britain to do to support the war effort. As John was in charge of the firm he had to stay and make sure the work was done well.

John's company had to build 'pre-fabricated' timber huts for the army. These huts were made in sections which were put together when they had been transported to the place where they were needed. They were taken by train all over the country. The Laing Company also helped to build a special army village in Scotland.

The company was already busy but then it was asked to do even more work. The newly invented aeroplane became important during the war. As aeroplanes were improved and made larger, faster and more powerful, they needed better runways. The aeroplanes also needed hangars – huge garages where the planes could be kept safely. The Laing Company was asked to build both runways and hangars. It was a difficult job to construct something so unusual and so big in a short time, but when the work was finished the Royal Flying Corps (later renamed the Royal Air Force) was delighted with the result.

At the end of the First World War John's company had grown. It had done a lot of extra work during the war, but in peacetime the armed forces didn't need timber huts or more runways. John now had to find new work to keep his employees busy.

The war had been a tragedy. Hundreds of thousands of young men had been killed. Millions of people had lost a member of their family. Homes and buildings had been damaged and neglected. This meant that new buildings and houses were needed, but because of the war, there was a shortage of skilled bricklayers. John worked with his designers to develop a new type of house made of concrete which was quicker and easier to construct than a

John Laing in uniform, during the First World War

brick building. These houses were called 'Easiform' houses and the Laing Company began to build them all over the country. John found that there was always more and more work to do. Each year more people began to work for the Laing Company and it continued to grow.

Even though they were so busy, John liked to check that all the building was being done well. He spent long hours travelling to all the different building sites to see the men and look at the work. If he saw people working hard he was satisfied, but he also had a quick temper. If he found anyone being lazy or a job done badly he would get angry. Sometimes, if he was not happy about the way a wall had been constructed, he would demand that it was knocked down and built again.

When John went to look around Easiform houses, he would imagine that he was going to live there himself. He made sure that the houses were comfortable: he checked to see that the doors would fit and there would be no draughts. He didn't want to sell people houses that he would not be happy to live in with his own family.

What Do You Think?

1. Why do you think John insisted that walls were knocked down and built again if he was not happy with them? What effect do you think this might have had on the workers?

2. When John inspected a house he imagined that his family was going to live in it. Suggest reasons why he did this.

3. What does the word 'perfectionist' mean? Is it good to have high standards? Can having high standards ever be a problem? Give reasons for your answer.

Good Deals for the Workers

As he visited all the different sites, John would try to get to know as many of his employees as he could. When he first worked for the business with his father, he knew everybody. Even when he was in charge of the company, John Laing would always find time to speak to everyone. It didn't matter if they were a manager or the newest apprentice. He expected all his employees to work hard and do a good job but he was also concerned about people.

In those days, builders did not have pensions or paid holidays. Everyone was expected to save up money for their old age. If they wanted to go on holiday, they would have to save up money and take unpaid time off work. John did not agree with this, so he invited his employees to join a 'shilling-a-week' scheme. Each week an employee could put aside a shilling (5p) from their wages and the company would put aside another shilling. (You could buy six loaves of bread for one shilling.) At the end of a year this money would pay for the employee's holiday.

John was also the first person to introduce pensions into the building industry. This meant that the company and the employee regularly put money aside until the employee became too old to work. Then they were able to live on these savings. The Laing Company didn't *have* to do this. It cost them money, but John wasn't only interested in the company making a profit, he also thought that treating people well was important.

One day John went to visit a busy building site. At that time they did not have motorized machinery, but sometimes the men would use hand-operated cranes to do some of the heavy jobs. Half-way round his tour of the site, John stopped to watch a man working one of these cranes. As he watched he noticed the man looked tired and worried. He went up to him and began to talk to him about the job. After a few minutes John said, 'Are you all right? You look very tired.'

'I am tired,' the man replied. 'My wife is seriously ill and the doctor says she must rest in bed. But while she's so ill I have to do everything at home. This morning I had to look after her and the children and do the cooking and cleaning before starting work here at 7 o'clock.'

John listened carefully to the crane-operator then walked on.

He decided to find out more about the man and went to visit his wife. She was very ill, just as the crane-operator had described. The same afternoon he went back to the man and said, 'I know you spoke the truth. Please go home for two weeks and look after your family. I will make sure that you are paid as usual.'

Everyone who worked for John knew that he was a Christian and that he went to church. At all times John tried to behave at work as a Christian should.

What Do You Think?

1. John cared about the people who worked for his company. How do you think this concern affected their lives?

2. Is there any evidence to show that conditions for working people have improved since 1900? If so, what is it? Do you think that big businesses care for their employees today?

3. If you had been John Laing, would you have set up pension and holiday schemes when you didn't have to? Give reasons for your answer.

Churches, Crusaders and Camps

By 1926 the Laing Company was doing very well and working on building sites all over the country. John could have been a rich man but he never forgot his 'Programme of Life', and he gave most of his money away.

> The public may enter and use the seats around the side of the garage during daylight

At this time the company moved its head office to north London. John chose a site for the new office, accommodation for office staff and a house for himself. He could have had a very big, glamorous house full of the latest luxuries, but instead he chose to build an ordinary house surrounded by views of the countryside. He put up a sign at the garden gate saying that anyone was welcome to sit in the garden to enjoy the views.

Once they had moved, John and his family missed the church and their friends in Carlisle. There were no similar churches near their new home and the family missed that style of worship. At first they had to travel a long way on Sundays to go to one of their churches, then John and some of his Christian friends decided it would be a good idea to build one nearer to the new houses in the area. So the Laing Company built a new church called Woodcroft Hall. John paid for two thirds of the cost of the building himself.

When the church opened it held services for adults and a Sunday school for children. Everyone was surprised by how many children wanted to go – soon there were over a thousand children attending the church on Sundays. The church buildings had to be extended twice and classes had to be repeated as the halls were still too small to hold all the children!

As part of his work for the church, John led a Crusader class. This was a meeting for young people who wanted to

Woodcroft Hall – the new church

learn about the Christian faith. They would also have quizzes and games.

In the summer John and Beatrice would go camping with Crusaders from classes all over the country. John allowed himself three weeks' holiday each year. Two of these weeks he would spend at Crusader camps, leading walks and organizing games, competitions and sports tournaments. Even when he became older John was always very energetic, and could often walk further and more quickly than any of the young people on the camp.

What Do You Think?

1. All through his working life John spent two out of the three weeks of his holidays helping out at youth camps. The work was fun, but also very demanding and tiring. What reasons might he have given for spending his holiday doing this?

2. Is being generous just about giving money? In what other ways can people be generous to others?

Another War

John held his breath as he listened to the Prime Minister's voice on the crackling radio. It was 3 September 1939. As everyone had feared, Britain and Germany were officially at war. In a few weeks' time John would be sixty but the following years were to be the busiest of his life. The company became involved in building aircraft factories and by the end of the war had constructed over sixty airfields.

As the German Nazi leader, Adolf Hitler, invaded more and more countries, it had seemed inevitable that Britain would have to fight him. So the British government and the armed forces had prepared for war. John won the contract to build a highly secret headquarters for RAF Bomber Command. It was to be constructed in the style of an ordinary village but with all the operation rooms deep underground, under the village itself. The village did not look special or important and all through the war it did not need to be camouflaged. John worked closely on all the different building processes. He talked at length with the architects who designed the complex and he was regularly on site to check that everything was done exactly right until it was completed in 1939.

Life during the Second World War was hard. Thousands of men went to fight and women began to work in factories to replace the men serving in the armed forces. For safety, many children living in the big cities were moved to the countryside, separated from their families. Many cities were bombed. In the six years of the war, one third of all houses in Britain were damaged or destroyed. Between the bomb attacks, the Laing Company did its best to repair as many houses as possible or at least make them safe.

The night of 15 November 1940 marked an important development in the war and was a devastating night for Coventry. During that one night, 449 German bombers flew over the city and dropped thousands of bombs. There were 568 people killed and hundreds more seriously injured. Many parts of the city were reduced to rubble – even the Cathedral was destroyed.

It is thought that the lead in the Cathedral roof had looked silvery in the moonlight and the bombers had mistaken it for a factory – one of their targets. They dropped bomb after bomb on to it.

Eleven hours after the air attack on the city began the sirens gave the 'all-clear' signal. Immediately a group of people from the Cathedral gathered together in its smouldering ruins. One of the men in charge of the Cathedral, Provost Howard, said, 'It will be rebuilt to the glory of God.' Someone else took two charred oak beams which had been part of the roof and tied them together to make a cross. He put this up in the middle of the chaos to remind them of the Christian message of forgiveness.

As the war raged, Cathedral staff and local people struggled to make Provost Howard's dream become reality. They organized building committees and discussed all sorts of ideas and plans for a new building. In 1954, long after the war had finished, they finally chose a design for the new Cathedral and a year later they asked John Laing's company to build it.

The company began this important work when John Laing was seventy-six years old. He saw this great opportunity as a highlight in the history of the company and a chance to use their experience to build a place of worship that would bring glory to God. John and his sons thought the work was a privilege and together they decided not to make any profit from it. This meant that only the cost of the materials and wages would have to be paid from Cathedral funds.

The best and most experienced workers were chosen to build the Cathedral. John wrote to them encouraging them to do their very best work and to use only the highest-quality materials – he wanted the building to survive for at least a thousand years.

The new Cathedral was completed in 1962, twenty-two years after the old one had been burnt to the ground. It is recognized around the world to be an architectural triumph and is a centre for reconciliation. Many people visit the Cathedral each year to admire the building, the workmanship and, of course, to worship God. Although few of the visitors realize it, it is also a permanent monument to the skill and generosity of John Laing, his sons and their company.

John and Beatrice Laing after the consecration of Coventry Cathedral in 1962

What Do You Think?

1. Although John was a Christian he was involved in building work for the armed forces. Why might some people find this puzzling?

2. Why did John think it was a privilege to work on Coventry Cathedral? Imagine you are a builder. What kind of building would you most like to create? Why would you enjoy working on it?

3. Have you ever had the chance to be involved in a project or event that has felt like a privilege? What is it that makes some work special?

Rich Man ... Poor Man?

After the Second World War, John Laing's company began to build Easiform houses again. Between 1945 and 1968 they built over 100 000 of these houses. John became well known for his skill and expertise in house building. As a result he was asked to advise both the British and the American government on their housing policies.

Kirby and Maurice, John's sons, both fought in the war. When they returned, John was sixty-six and wanted them to take over running the business. He did not intend to retire completely but knew it was time to hand over more responsibility to his sons. He remained closely involved with the company and the building projects for many more years.

The company had grown beyond all recognition since the time when John had started working for his own father as an apprentice. By 1950 it employed 15 000 people and was still expanding quickly. It was doing building work throughout Britain and was beginning to take on projects all over the world.

Throughout his life, John was never too busy to go to church or meet with other Christians to pray and talk. He divided his time equally between his business and Christian interests. John always remembered the promise he had made to God in Barrow-in-Furness about his life and his money. Even though he could have been a very rich man, John chose to give his money away. Yet he kept this a secret, because in the Bible it says:

> When you give away money to the poor, do not let your left hand find out what your right hand is doing.
>
> (MATTHEW 6:3)

This means that Christians should not give away money to impress other people, instead they should give it away privately so that only God knows about it. To make sure that his giving was a secret, John put large amounts of money into an anonymous charitable fund which gave away his money in the way he wanted. Lots of churches, missionaries and other organizations have received money from this fund. Many may never have known that the money came from John Laing.

In establishing his business, John always considered training to be very important. He thought this was true for Christians too and that they should have a special college to study in. He quietly provided most of the money to build and establish the London Bible College. Hundreds of Christians from different parts of the Christian Church from Britain and abroad now attend the College every year to learn more about the Bible. Some want to become ministers, some missionaries. Other students simply want to know more about the Bible and the Christian life. Most students don't know that the College exists because of a gift from a rich man who chose to give his money away. Like so many of the other generous things John did, he wanted this to be a secret.

In September 1959, at the age of eighty, John Laing attended the official opening of the first section of the M1 Motorway. The Laing Company had been asked to construct it because they had gained so much experience making runways during the war. The first section of the motorway, just over eighty kilometres long, was built between Dunstable and Rugby. Despite his age John was involved in the contract and watched the creation of the road with interest and pride. When he had been at school, cars were being invented, they were only a dream; it is amazing to think that in his old age John saw his own company build Britain's first major motorway.

After a long, busy, happy life John Laing died in 1978 at the age of ninety-eight. He had made millions of pounds and he had chosen to give most of this money away. When he died he owned only £371, probably less than most of the people who had worked for him. His love for God was more important to him than money and his life had proved it.

John Laing (right), aged nearly eighty, visiting the M1 Motorway site

What Do You Think?

1. John wanted to keep all his acts of generosity a secret. What reasons do you think he would have given for this?

2. Think of something kind or generous you have done recently. Did you tell anyone about it? Do you think it was hard for John to keep his kindness a secret? Which passage in the Bible did he think of when he secretly helped to found the London Bible College?

3. When John Laing's company started building the M1, cars were seen as an important form of transport and motorways were regarded as a great invention. Make a list of all the advantages of motorway travel as seen in 1959.

Today many people have different views. They claim that there are too many cars on the roads. Suggest three present-day arguments (a) for and (b) against motorway travel.

4. John handed over a successful business to his sons but gave most of his money away. Do you think old people should hand on their wealth to their families? Give reasons. If someone expects to benefit from a relative's will, how might this affect their plans for the future?

Biographical Notes

John Laing was born in Carlisle, Cumbria, in 1879. He left school when he was fifteen and started to work in his father's building company. In 1909 the company nearly became bankrupt and a short time later John wrote his 'Programme of Life', promising to live a Christian life and give away any money he didn't really need. In 1910 he married Beatrice Harland. They had two sons, Kirby and Maurice.

The Laing Company began to expand during the First World War. This growth continued after the war, when it began to build Easiform houses. In 1938 the company built the secret RAF Bomber Command Headquarters and during the Second World War constructed over sixty airfields. In 1955, the company began to build Coventry Cathedral. Four years later, in 1959, John Laing received a knighthood and during the same year the company completed the first stretch of the M1 Motorway. John died in 1978, aged ninety-eight, having secretly given away almost all the money he had made to many different people and charitable organizations.

Things to Do

1 Imagine that you are a journalist. Following the death of John Laing, your editor has asked you to write an obituary (brief details about his life) for the newspaper. Write 100 words on what John did and another 100 words about what kind of man he was, what he thought was important and what he believed.

2 Work in pairs. One of you is a radio reporter and one of you is John Laing. The reporter is interviewing John to help listeners understand why he has chosen to give so much money away during his life. Make a tape-recording of the interview.

3 Imagine you have earned or inherited £1000. Write down (a) how you would spend it and (b) how you think John Laing would have spent it.

4 Look up the definition of the word 'generosity'. Using this book, list all the people and organizations who benefited from John Laing's generosity.

5 Write a conversation between a person who has worked for John Laing's company for twenty years and a new member of staff. The older employee is trying to explain to the new one how the company pension and holiday schemes work. Think about the questions someone who hasn't worked for John Laing before might want to ask about the company.

6 Some employers thought that John Laing was being foolish when he tried to improve life for his employees. Write or record a conversation between John and an owner of another company. John is doing his best to explain that it is sensible to care for the needs of workers. How does he persuade the other person to think about their workforce?

7 Look through the business sections of modern newspapers and cut out articles about company directors and working conditions generally. Make them into two posters, one which reminds you of John Laing and his company and one that represents opposite values. You could also include news items on disputes at work.

8 Research into New Testament teachings about attitudes towards money, e.g. Matthew 6:1–4, 22:15–22, Mark 12:41–44 and 1 Timothy 6:6–10. Write a report on your findings.

9 Choose a charity and find out who or what it supports and how it raises money. Design a poster encouraging others to help your chosen charity.

10 Imagine you are an older person writing to congratulate a newly married couple. Put the saying 'Don't let the sun go down on your anger' in your letter and explain to the bride and groom what it means.

11 Design your own public building. It could be a place of worship for a religious tradition you have studied or a college or school. Explain what symbols you would want to put in this building to encourage people to live together in harmony or to show the values the community who will use it think are important.

12 Imagine you are the Very Important Person making a speech at the opening of **either** the M1 **or** the London Bible College. Deliver your speech to the class, telling them something about your hopes for the project.

13 Research the life and work of other employers who have tried to improve life for working people, e.g. the Cadbury family or the Leverhulmes.

14 Create an advertisement seeking a person to help with a youth group. Your advertisement should explain what the person will have to do and that they will not be paid for their time. How are you going to attract volunteers? Include some advantages of doing this job in your advertisement.

15 Ask some adults what they think are good working conditions. Ask them for their reasons. Can you add any of your own? Write a report of your findings. Say why you think employers should provide those working conditions.

Questions for Assessment or Examination Candidates

16 Write a mini-biography of John Laing and explain how he followed the teachings of Jesus in both his work and his leisure time.

17 Using examples from a religious tradition you have studied, show how the teachings of religious leaders encourage the wealthy to assist those who are less fortunate.

18 Answer **one** of the following structured essays:

(a) Explain with examples the difference between 'charity' and 'a charity'. (5 marks)

(b) In what ways did John Laing follow the commandment to love your neighbour? (10 marks)

(c) 'The employer's first duty is the welfare of company employees.' What evidence is there to show that John Laing agreed with this statement? (5 marks)

OR

(a) Do you think that John Laing provides a good role-model for modern employers? Give reasons for your answer. (5 marks)

(b) In your opinion was John Laing a good Christian? Support your argument with examples from his life. (10 marks)

(c) Select passages from the New Testament and show how John Laing followed their teachings. (5 marks)

Religious and Moral Education Press
*An imprint of Chansitor Publications Ltd,
a wholly owned subsidiary of
Hymns Ancient & Modern Ltd
St Mary's Works, St Mary's Plain
Norwich, Norfolk NR3 3BH*

Copyright © 1998 Deborah Helme

Deborah Helme has asserted her right under the Copyright, Designs and Patents Act, 1988, to be identified as Author of this Work.

All rights reserved. No part of this publication may be reproduced, stored in a retrieval system, or transmitted, in any form or by any means, electronic, electrostatic, magnetic tape, mechanical, photocopying, recording or otherwise, without permission in writing from the publishers.

First published 1998

ISBN 1 85175 158 0

Designed and typeset by
TOPICS – The Creative Partnership,
Exeter

Printed in Great Britain by
Brightsea Press, Exeter for
Chansitor Publications Ltd, Norwich

Notes for Teachers

The first Faith in Action books were published in the late 1970s and the series has remained popular with both teachers and pupils. However, much in education has changed over the last twenty years, such as the development of both new examination syllabuses in Religious Studies and local agreed syllabuses for Religious Education which place more emphasis on pupils' own understanding, interpretation and evaluation of religious belief and practice, rather than a simple knowledge of events. This has encouraged us to amend the style of the Faith in Action Series to make it more suitable for today's classroom.

The aim is, as before, to tell the stories of people who have lived and acted according to their faith, but we have included alongside the main story questions which will encourage pupils to think about the reasons for the behaviour of our main characters and to empathize with the situations in which they found themselves. We hope that pupils will also be able to relate some of the issues in the stories to other issues in modern society, either in their own area or on a global scale.

The 'What Do You Think?' questions may be used for group or class discussion or for short written exercises. The 'Things to Do' at the end of the story include ideas for longer activities and more-structured questions suitable for assessment or examination practice.

In line with current syllabus requirements, as Britain is a multifaith society, Faith in Action characters will be selected from a wide variety of faith backgrounds and many of the questions may be answered from the perspective of more than one faith.

CMB, 1997

Acknowledgements
This book has been published under the auspices of the Stapleford Project. The Project produces materials and offers in-service courses to resource the teaching of Christianity in schools. Full details of courses and publications are available from The Stapleford Centre, Wesley Place, Stapleford, Nottingham NG9 8DP.

The publishers would like to thank the Laing family for their permission to use the photographs reproduced in this book. Every effort has been made to contact copyright owners and the publishers apologize to any whose rights have inadvertently not been acknowledged.